Celebrity Bios

MICHAEL B. JORDAN

Keli Sipperley

WWW.APEXEDITIONS.COM

Copyright © 2025 by Apex Editions, Mendota Heights, MN 55120. All rights reserved. No part of this book may be reproduced or utilized in any form or by any means without written permission from the publisher.

Apex is distributed by North Star Editions:
sales@northstareditions.com | 888-417-0195

Produced for Apex by Red Line Editorial.

Photographs ©: Sthanlee B. Mirador/Sipa USA/AP Images, cover, 1; Pictorial Press Ltd/Alamy, 4–5; Shutterstock Images, 6–7, 8–9, 10–11, 12–13, 14–15, 24–25, 30–31, 34–35, 37, 38–39, 40–41, 42–43, 46–47, 49, 52–53, 58; Lance Staedler/Paramount Pictures/Getty Images Entertainment/Getty Images, 16–17; Michael Loccisano/FilmMagic/Getty Images, 18–19; Alberto E. Rodriguez/Getty Images Entertainment/Getty Images, 20–21; Stephen Lovekin/FilmMagic/Getty Images, 22–23; Michael Tullberg/Getty Images Entertainment/Getty Images, 26–27; Jordan Strauss/Invision/AP Images, 28–29; Red Line Editorial, 32–33; PictureLux/The Hollywood Archive/Alamy, 44–45; Chris Polk/VMN18/Getty Images Entertainment/Getty Images, 50–51; J. C. Olivera/Getty Images Entertainment/Getty Images, 54–55; Rich Fury/Getty Images Entertainment/Getty Images, 56–57

Library of Congress Control Number: 2023922408

ISBN
979-8-89250-217-7 (hardcover)
979-8-89250-238-2 (paperback)
979-8-89250-278-8 (book pdf)
979-8-89250-259-7 (hosted ebook)

Printed in the United States of America
Mankato, MN
082024

NOTE TO PARENTS AND EDUCATORS

Apex books are designed to build literacy skills in striving readers. Exciting, high-interest content attracts and holds readers' attention. The text is carefully leveled to allow students to achieve success quickly.

TABLE OF CONTENTS

Chapter 1
THROWING PUNCHES 4

Chapter 2
FROM BASKETBALL TO ACTING 9

Chapter 3
TV TIME 16

Chapter 4
BIGGER ROLES 26

In the Spotlight
LASTING IMPACT 36

Chapter 5
MAJOR MOVIE STAR 38

In the Spotlight
THE PERFECT CAMEO 48

Chapter 6
LIFTING UP OTHERS 51

FAST FACTS • 59
COMPREHENSION QUESTIONS • 60
GLOSSARY • 62
TO LEARN MORE • 63
ABOUT THE AUTHOR • 63
INDEX • 64

Chapter 1

THROWING PUNCHES

Michael B. Jordan's fists fly. He swings with power. Around him, lights shine. Cameras follow every move. Jordan is working on a movie set. His character, Adonis Creed, is a boxer. Creed is fighting a strong rival.

Filmmakers wanted the fights in *Creed* to look realistic.

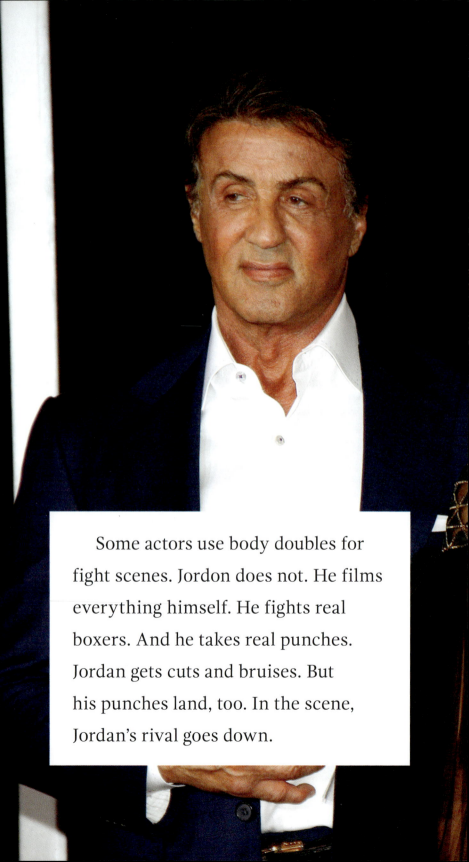

Some actors use body doubles for fight scenes. Jordon does not. He films everything himself. He fights real boxers. And he takes real punches. Jordan gets cuts and bruises. But his punches land, too. In the scene, Jordan's rival goes down.

Michael B. Jordan acted alongside Tessa Thompson (center) and Sylvester Stallone (left) in *Creed*.

BECOMING CREED

Jordan worked hard to become Creed. He trained for months. He practiced boxing and worked out. Jordan gained 24 pounds (11 kg) of muscle for the role.

Newark is the biggest city in New Jersey. It is near New York City.

Chapter 2

FROM BASKETBALL TO ACTING

Michael Bakari Jordan was born on February 9, 1987. At first, his family lived in California. But they moved when Michael was two. They went to Newark, New Jersey. Michael grew up there. He was close to family. And he loved playing basketball.

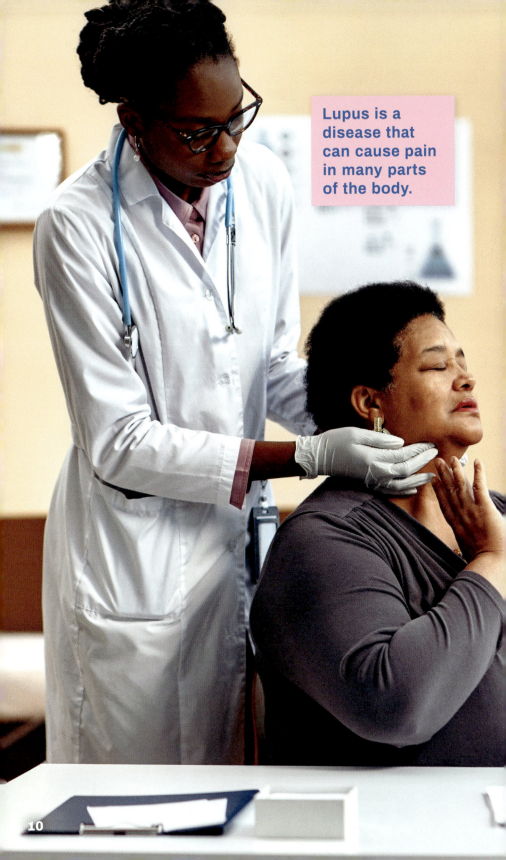

Lupus is a disease that can cause pain in many parts of the body.

When Michael was young, his mother was sick. Doctors said she had a disease called lupus. One day, Michael went to the doctor with her. An office worker noticed Michael. She explained that her sons were models. She thought Michael should model, too.

Michael's mother was interested in the idea. Modeling jobs could help pay for college. At first, Michael wasn't sure. He just wanted to play ball. But he agreed to try. So, Michael started going to photo shoots. He appeared in ads for local stores.

NAME WITH FAME

At school, some classmates teased Michael. They compared him to basketball superstar Michael Jordan. The teasing made Michael work harder. He wanted to be great, too.

Michael appeared in ads for stores such as Toys "R" Us.

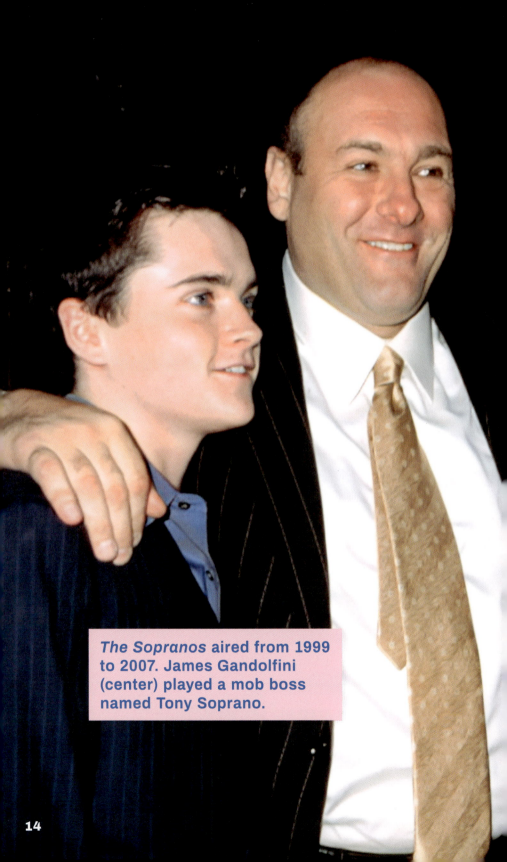

The Sopranos aired from 1999 to 2007. James Gandolfini (center) played a mob boss named Tony Soprano.

Michael's manager soon had a new idea. The manager asked if Michael wanted to try acting. A year and a half later, Michael began earning small TV roles. In 1999, he appeared in a famous TV show. He played a bully on *The Sopranos*. His role was tiny. It lasted just one episode. And Michael was onscreen for only 30 seconds. Even so, it was a good start.

THE SOPRANOS

The Sopranos was a popular crime drama. The show was about a mob boss. It followed his crimes and problems in his personal life. *The Sopranos* ran for six seasons. It won more than 100 awards.

Chapter 3
TV TIME

In 1999, Michael's first film came out. The movie was called *Black & White*. Michael's part was tiny. His character didn't even have a name. In 2001, he got another movie role. He played a baseball player in *Hardball*. His role was small again. But this time, his character had a name.

Hardball is about a young baseball team in Chicago.

Michael's character appeared in 13 episodes of *The Wire*.

In 2002, Michael got his big break. He was cast as Wallace in *The Wire*. Wallace was in a gang. He did crimes. Later, he tried to make things right. Playing Wallace changed Michael. He learned to lose himself in his character. He fell in love with acting.

A WELL-LOVED SHOW

The Wire aired on HBO from 2002 to 2008. Viewers and critics loved it. Some TV writers called it the greatest show ever made. In the 2020s, many people still thought that.

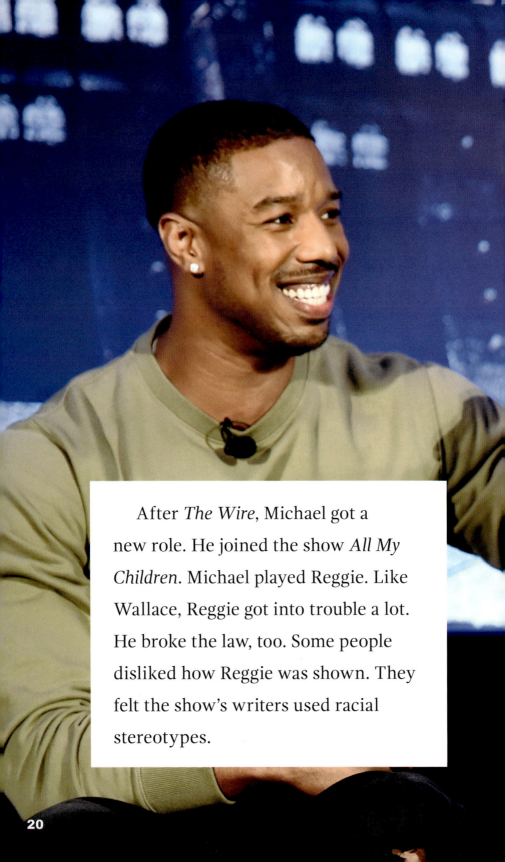

After *The Wire*, Michael got a new role. He joined the show *All My Children*. Michael played Reggie. Like Wallace, Reggie got into trouble a lot. He broke the law, too. Some people disliked how Reggie was shown. They felt the show's writers used racial stereotypes.

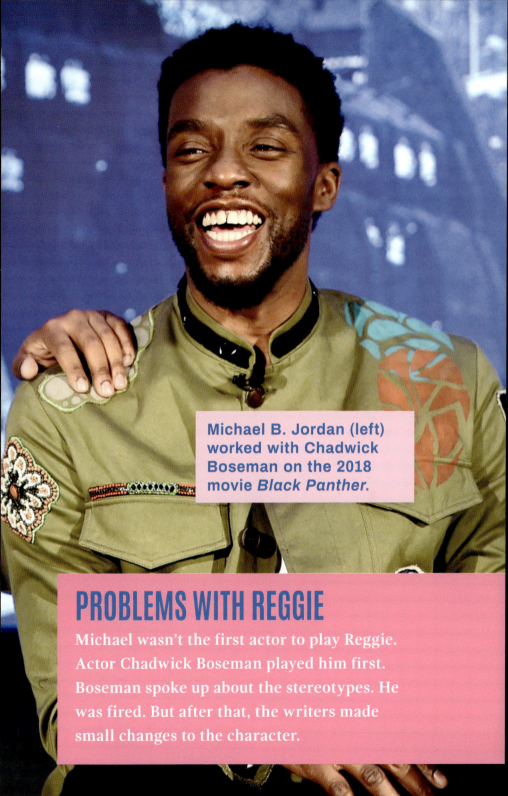

Michael B. Jordan (left) worked with Chadwick Boseman on the 2018 movie *Black Panther*.

PROBLEMS WITH REGGIE

Michael wasn't the first actor to play Reggie. Actor Chadwick Boseman played him first. Boseman spoke up about the stereotypes. He was fired. But after that, the writers made small changes to the character.

21

Michael attends an awards show with *All My Children* co-star Alexa Havins in 2004.

Michael filmed *All My Children* for three years, from 2003 to 2006. During that time, he was still in high school. He went to Newark Arts High School. Michael also played basketball.

A JOB WELL DONE

Michael tried hard to play Reggie. He wanted to show Reggie was more than a stereotype. He was even nominated for an award. But later, Michael made a decision. He did not want to play characters like that anymore.

Hollywood has been the center of the US film industry for more than 100 years.

Michael B. Jordan graduated from high school in 2005. He wanted to have a film career. So, in 2006, he moved to Los Angeles, California. Jordan hoped the move would help him land bigger jobs. He also wanted to play new kinds of characters. His big TV roles had all been criminals. Jordan wanted his movie roles to be different.

HOLLYWOOD

Hollywood is an area of Los Angeles. The US film industry is based there. Many movies are made there. Many producers and directors live there, too.

Chapter 4

BIGGER ROLES

Jordan didn't act in Hollywood films right away. But in 2009, he scored another big TV role. He played Vince on *Friday Night Lights*. Vince, a high school quarterback, was not a simple character. He grew and changed over time. Jordan portrayed that journey well. He showed his acting range.

Jordan (second from left) attends an event with football players and actors in 2010.

In 2012, Jordan co-starred in *Chronicle*. It was a science fiction movie. Jordan played a boy named Steve. Steve and his friends find a strange item. It gives them superpowers. The movie had a low budget. It didn't include famous stars. But it was a surprise hit.

Jordan (right) appeared in the film *Red Tails* in 2012. He and his castmates played a group of African American pilots in World War II (1939–1945).

LOOKING REAL

Chronicle is a found-footage film. In this style, stories are made up. But the shots make it seem like events are real. For example, characters may hold cameras.

Fruitvale Station is named after a real station in Oakland, California. It is where Oscar Grant was killed.

Jordan's first leading movie role came in 2013. *Fruitvale Station* was based on a true story. Police officers shot Oscar Grant in 2009. The film shows the 24 hours before Grant's death. A small company made the film. But it won many awards. So, many viewers went to see it. It became a surprise hit.

MAN WITH A MISSION

Jordan had a goal for *Fruitvale Station*. He wanted people to think about how they treat others. He succeeded. The film got more people talking about racial profiling.

Marvel has been making comic books about the Fantastic Four since 1961.

In 2015, Jordan starred in *Fantastic Four*. He played the superhero Johnny Storm, the Human Torch. The film was based on Marvel comics. But it didn't get good reviews. Around this time, Jordan also acted in *That Awkward Moment*. Most critics didn't like this comedy. But some fans did. It made them laugh.

BREAKING BARRIERS

Some people didn't want Jordan to play Johnny Storm. In the comics, the character is white. Some people felt the actor should be white, too. But Jordan wanted people to see a new version of Storm.

33

Jordan bounced back with another major role in 2015. He landed the title role in *Creed*. Ryan Coogler wrote and directed the movie. It was Jordan's second time working with him. Coogler had also written and directed *Fruitvale Station*.

ROCKY

Creed was related to the *Rocky* films. Those movies are about a Philadelphia boxer. Adonis Creed is the son of Rocky's rival.

In the *Rocky* movies, Sylvester Stallone (center) plays Rocky. Rocky becomes Creed's trainer in *Creed*.

In the Spotlight

LASTING IMPACT

Fruitvale Station covers serious topics. And it's based on a real person. Jordan felt honored to play Oscar Grant. He wanted to do it carefully and correctly. So, Jordan worked very hard. Jordan connected with Grant's family and friends. They told Jordan about Grant. Jordan tried to show his characteristics. He even wore Grant's clothes.

Jordan said making the movie changed his life. And he hoped watching it would impact people, too.

Oscar Grant's death angered many people. They protested on the streets.

Chapter 5
MAJOR MOVIE STAR

reed was a massive success. It made more than $170 million worldwide. Audiences loved it. They wanted more movies with the character. So, Jordan starred in a sequel. *Creed II* came out in 2018.

Creed II was even more popular than the first movie. The film made more than $210 million in theaters.

Fahrenheit 451 played at the Cannes Film Festival in 2018.

That same year, Jordan appeared in *Fahrenheit 451*. This movie was based on a book by Ray Bradbury. Jordan played a firefighter. But his character didn't put out fires. Instead, he set fires. He burned books. He wanted to limit knowledge.

BOOK TO MOVIE

In 2019, Jordan starred in *Just Mercy*. The film is about lawyer Bryan Stevenson. He defends a man sentenced to death. The film was based on Stevenson's own writing.

Jordan also did another film with Coogler. Coogler was making a movie called *Black Panther*. It was about a Marvel superhero. Coogler wanted Jordan to play Erik Killmonger. This character has a long history. He has appeared in Marvel comics since the 1970s. Killmonger often fights against heroes. Jordan accepted the role.

He became the first person to play Killmonger in a live-action film.

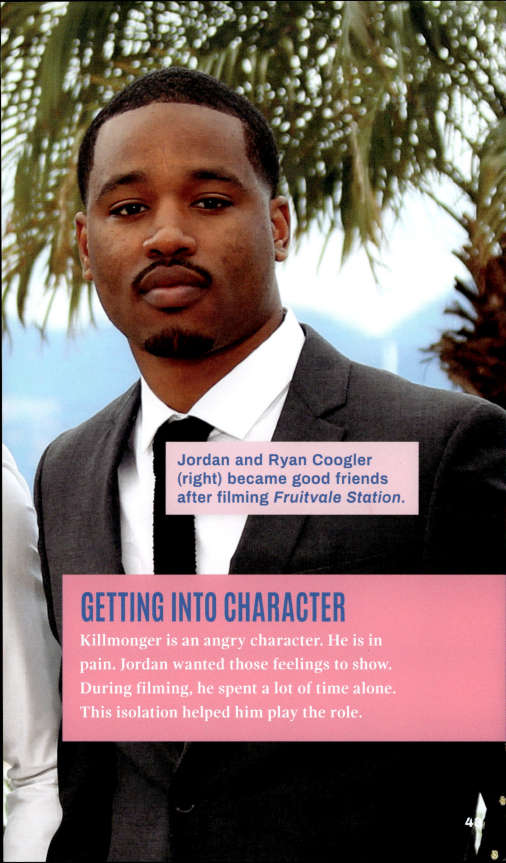

Jordan and Ryan Coogler (right) became good friends after filming *Fruitvale Station*.

GETTING INTO CHARACTER

Killmonger is an angry character. He is in pain. Jordan wanted those feelings to show. During filming, he spent a lot of time alone. This isolation helped him play the role.

Black Panther came out in 2018. It was a massive hit. Audiences around the world loved it. It earned more than $1 billion in its first four weeks. Jordan's character was a big part of the buzz. Viewers enjoyed how Jordan played the villain.

In *Black Panther*, Erik Killmonger (right) travels to the nation of Wakanda. He wants to become king.

BECOMING KILLMONGER

Killmonger is covered in bumpy scars. He gets one each time he kills. Four makeup artists applied the bumps to Jordan's skin. They had to reapply them every day of filming. Each time took hours.

Jordan and Tessa Thompson attend a showing of *Creed III*.

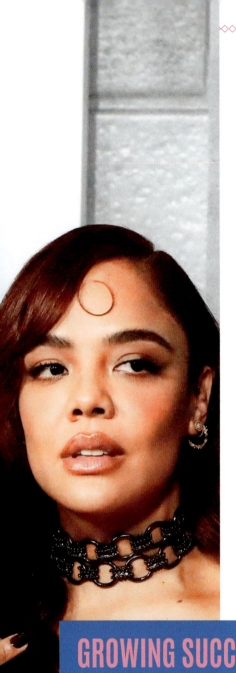

Next, Jordan made a third Creed movie. *Creed III* came out in 2023. Once again, Jordan had the lead role. But this time, Jordan took on an extra job. He directed the film. Jordan hadn't directed before. But he had watched and learned from other directors. This work paid off. The film was another big success.

GROWING SUCCESS

The first *Creed* movie did well. But *Creed*'s sequels grew the series even more. By 2023, the three films had earned more than $660 million.

In the Spotlight

THE PERFECT CAMEO

In 2021, Jordan appeared in *Space Jam: A New Legacy*. It was a sequel to the 1996 movie *Space Jam*. That first film starred basketball legend Michael Jordan.

In *A New Legacy*, a character mentions Michael Jordan. He says Michael Jordan is watching their game. Then the camera shows the crowd. Michael B. Jordan sits there. He is eating popcorn. The playful cameo worked. People recognized Jordan and got the joke. His dream as a kid had come true. He was famous himself.

Michael Jordan played for the Chicago Bulls. He was one of the greatest basketball players ever.

In 2018, Jordan won an MTV Movie and TV Award for Best Villain.

Chapter 6

LIFTING UP OTHERS

Jordan has played a wide variety of characters. People connect with his characters. He is considered one of the best modern actors. And he earned a star on the Hollywood Walk of Fame.

Jordan often attends events with his family. He has said his mom is his superhero.

Jordan often uses his fame to help others. For example, Jordan helps people with lupus. His mother inspired him to do that. Jordan hosts an event called MBJAM. The event raises money for lupus research. It also helps spread awareness about the disease.

DREAM HOUSE

Family is important to Jordan. He once dreamed of buying his parents a home. In 2015, he did. For a while, Jordan lived there, too. He could afford to buy his own house. But he liked being near his parents.

53

Jordan has also worked to make Hollywood more inclusive. During his career, he saw people of color get fewer roles and opportunities than others. Jordan wanted to change that. So, he formed his own company in 2016. It's called Outlier Society Productions. The company hires actors from many different backgrounds. It works with diverse storytellers, too.

Elizabeth Raposo (left) became president of Outlier Society in 2021.

TRYING ROLES

Jordan noticed that few roles were made for Black actors. So, he tried out for characters that were originally described as white. That included his role in *Chronicle*. His character in *Without Remorse* was white in the book, too.

Outlier Society's first project was *Fahrenheit 451*. The company also produced *Creed III* and *A Journal for Jordan*. It was a true story about a soldier writing to his son. The company tries to spotlight stories that are not told often. Jordan has had many great opportunities in his career. Now, he gives other people opportunities, too.

MORE PROJECTS

In 2019, Outlier Society began partnering with Amazon. The two companies made movies and TV series together. Outlier's content also streamed on Amazon Prime Video.

Jordan spoke at a protest in 2020. He called for film companies to hire and support Black workers.

FAST FACTS

Full name: Michael Bakari Jordan

Birth date: February 9, 1987

Birthplace: Santa Ana, California, United States of America

TIMELINE

1987 — Michael B. Jordan is born on February 9.

1999 — Michael appears on an episode of *The Sopranos*.

2002 — Michael plays Wallace in *The Wire*.

2003–06 — Michael plays Reggie on *All My Children*.

2009 — Michael B. Jordan joins the cast of *Friday Night Lights* as Vince.

2013 — Jordan lands his first leading role in the film *Fruitville Station*.

2015 — Jordan stars in the first *Creed* film.

2016 — Jordan forms his own production company, Outlier Society Productions.

2018 — Jordan plays Eric Killmonger in *Black Panther*.

2023 — Jordan directs for the first time with *Creed III*.

COMPREHENSION QUESTIONS

Write your answers on a separate piece of paper.

1. Write a few sentences that describe how Michael B. Jordan started acting.

2. Would you like to have the same name as a famous person? Why or why not?

3. Which movie was based on a true story?

   A. *Fruitvale Station*

   B. *Fahrenheit 451*

   C. *Hardball*

4. How could watching other directors help Jordan learn to direct?

   A. He could see what choices they made and what worked well.

   B. He could not do anything that other directors did.

   C. He could learn which actors are best.

5. What does **isolation** mean in this book?

*During filming, he spent a lot of time alone. This **isolation** helped him play the role.*

    A. going to large parties

    B. staying away from other people

    C. staying close to other people

6. What does **diverse** mean in this book?

*The company hires actors from many different backgrounds. It works with **diverse** storytellers, too.*

    A. all exactly the same

    B. coming from just one group

    C. coming from many different groups

Answer key on page 64.

GLOSSARY

body doubles
People who take actors' places in some scenes. They usually look similar to the actors they replace.

cameo
A short appearance in a movie or show, often done by a famous person.

critics
People who judge works of art such as movies and music.

directors
People who lead the making of movies.

inclusive
Trying to include as many different types of people as possible.

live-action
When characters are played by real people instead of being cartoons.

manager
A person who helps actors and models find work.

producers
People who help plan the making of movies or TV shows.

racial profiling
Suspecting or targeting a person based on their skin color or appearance.

stereotypes
Overly simple and harmful ideas about members of a certain group.

TO LEARN MORE

BOOKS

Burling, Alexis. *Hollywood*. Minneapolis: Abdo Publishing, 2020.

Huddleston, Emma. *Chadwick Boseman*. Mendota Heights, MN: Focus Readers, 2021.

London, Martha. *Chris Hemsworth*. Mendota Heights, MN: Focus Readers, 2021.

ONLINE RESOURCES

Visit **www.apexeditions.com** to find links and resources related to this title.

ABOUT THE AUTHOR

Keli Sipperley lives in Tampa, Florida, with her four children and two rowdy dogs. She is the author of more than 100 fiction and nonfiction books for kids published under multiple pen names.

INDEX

All My Children, 20–21, 23

Black & White, 16
Black Panther, 42–45
Boseman, Chadwick, 21

Chronicle, 28–29, 55
Coogler, Ryan, 34, 42
Creed, 4, 6–7, 34, 38, 47
Creed II, 38, 47
Creed III, 47, 56

directing, 25, 34, 47

Fahrenheit 451, 41, 56
Fantastic Four, 33
Friday Night Lights, 26
Fruitvale Station, 31, 34, 36

Hardball, 16
Hollywood, 25, 26, 51, 54

Jordan, Michael, 12, 48
Just Mercy, 41

Killmonger, 42–45

lupus, 11, 53

MBJAM, 53
modeling, 11–12

Outlier Society Productions, 54, 56

Sopranos, The, 15
Space Jam: A New Legacy, 48
Storm, Johnny, 32–33

Wire, The, 19–20
Without Remorse, 55

ANSWER KEY:

1. Answers will vary; 2. Answers will vary; 3. A; 4. A; 5. B; 6. C